# I Have a Dream

# *I Have a Dream*

## THE LIFE AND WORDS OF MARTIN LUTHER KING, JR.

### *by Jim Haskins*

THE MILLBROOK PRESS
BROOKFIELD, CONNECTICUT

Excerpts from *Stride Toward Freedom* by Martin Luther King, Jr. Copyright © 1958 by Martin Luther King, Jr. Copyright renewed © 1986 by Coretta Scott King, Dexter King, Martin Luther King, III, Yolanda King, Bernice King. Reprinted by permission of HarperCollins Publishers. Excerpt from "Letter from Birmingham Jail" from *Why We Can't Wait* by Martin Luther King, Jr. Copyright © 1963, 1964 by Martin Luther King, Jr. Copyright renewed © 1991 by Coretta Scott King. Reprinted by permission of HarperCollins Publishers. Excerpts from "My Trip to the Land of Gandhi," "I've Been to the Mountaintop," and "Nobel Prize Acceptance Speech" reprinted by permission of Joan Daves Agency, copyright © 1959 by Martin Luther King, Jr. Excerpts from "The Time for Freedom Has Come" and "I Have a Dream" reprinted by permission of Joan Daves Agency, copyright © 1961, 1976 by Martin Luther King, Jr.

Library of Congress Cataloging-in-Publication Data
Haskins, James, 1941–
I have a dream : the life and words of Martin Luther King, Jr. / by Jim Haskins.
p.    cm.
Includes bibliographical references (p.   ) and index.
Summary: Presents the life, words, and principles of the noted civil rights worker through extensive quotations from his speeches and writings.
ISBN 1-56294-087-2 (lib. bdg.)
1. King, Martin Luther, Jr., 1929–1968—Juvenile literature.   2. King, Martin Luther, Jr., 1929–1968—Quotations—Juvenile literature.   3. Afro-Americans—Civil rights—Juvenile literature.   4. Civil rights movements—United States—History—20th century—Juvenile literature.   5. Afro-Americans—Biography—Juvenile literature.   6. Civil rights workers—United States—Biography—Juvenile literature.   7. Baptists—United States—Clergy—Biography—Juvenile literature.   [1. King, Martin Luther, Jr., 1929–1968.   2. Civil rights workers.   3. Clergy.   4. Afro-Americans—Biography.]   I. King, Martin Luther, Jr., 1929–1968.   II. Title.
E185.97.K5H32   1992          323'.092—dc20          [B]   91-42528   CIP   AC

# Contents

*I am grateful to
Kathy Benson, Lisa Crawley,
Ann Kalkhoff, and Bill Rice
for their help.*

*To M.E. and E.B.*

# Introduction

## by Rosa Parks

I met Dr. Martin Luther King, Jr., for the first time in August 1955. He had been invited to be the guest speaker at the Montgomery branch NAACP meeting in Alabama. I was secretary of the branch. He had already arrived when I came in a few minutes early to set up for the meeting. We spoke to each other without introducing ourselves. I thought he was a college student. When the other members came in, Dr. King was introduced as the new pastor of the Dexter Avenue Baptist Church. I was surprised. He looked younger to me than his twenty-five years.

The meeting was opened, and after the usual business was finished, Dr. King gave us a brief but eloquent and interesting message. We were all very favorably impressed. I was amazed and pleased to hear such a young man deliver a really great message that was timely and much needed by us in Montgomery. He did not use notes or a prepared text. Someone next to me said, "Listen to that, he is something, isn't he?" I later learned that he was the husband of the beautiful and talented classical singer, Coretta Scott King. She had appeared on some musical programs that I had attended.

They were reluctant about living in the South. As southerners, they knew about legally enforced racial segregation, and they did not wish their children to suffer from its cruel brutality.

And yet, Dr. King preached to the Dexter Avenue Baptist Church Congregation. He accepted the pastorate of Dexter in March 1954, preached his first sermon as pastor that May, and moved to Montgomery in July.

Their first child, Yolanda Denise, called Yoki, was born November 17, 1955, two weeks before my arrest on a Montgomery bus. I was arrested on the Cleveland Avenue Bus, December 1, 1955, for refusing to give my seat to a white male passenger as ordered by the bus driver.

After my release from jail, with the help of Mr. E. D. Nixon, who posted my bond, and Attorney and Mrs. Clifford Durr, who were told exactly what the charges against me were (the officials would not tell Mr. Nixon the charges), I rode home with my husband, Raymond, and his friend, Mr. Mose Bishop, who drove the car. My mother, Leona McCauley, was anxiously waiting for us. We discussed my arrest, and I agreed to be a test case—protesting racial segregation in the transportation system. Mr. Nixon telephoned several persons, including Reverend Ralph Abernathy and Reverend M. L. King, Jr., who agreed that a meeting on the matter could be held at the Dexter Avenue Baptist Church, Friday evening, December 2.

The news about my trial and the beginning of the protest spread quickly. It was announced in the churches; it was publicized in the newspapers; and leaflets were passed out asking people not to ride the buses on Monday, December 5th. Other factors contributed to the success of the protest, but the buses were almost one hundred percent empty on December 5. People shared rides, took cabs, or walked to my trial. There were so many people, I almost could not get in the courthouse myself.

Later in the day after my trial, a meeting was held and the Montgomery Improvement Association (MIA) was formed. Reverend Abernathy suggested the name of the organization and Dr. King was chosen to be president.

Dr. King was so busy with the bus protest that when I asked him when his baby had been born, he could not remember her birth date. He said, "She was born three Thursdays ago."

He said that he wished to spend more time with his wife and little daughter; however, he was willing to give up his personal happiness to work for the success of the bus protest.

In the months and years that followed, he sacrificed much of his personal life for the movement. He inspired and motivated many people to accept nonviolence as their way of life. People who would never have considered turning the other cheek were willing to be trained in nonviolence under the leadership of Dr. King.

It seemed as if every time he spoke, he said something I wanted or needed to hear. After we listened to one of his messages, we were empowered to continue. His charisma and appeal continued to move me until his death.

The last time I saw Dr. King alive was the evening of March 21, 1968. I went to a program with Shelton and Louise Tappes. Dr. King's appearance was sponsored by a women's organization in an affluent suburb of Detroit, Michigan. There were so many people, it was difficult to find a seat. A large group of hostile white people was milling around as we entered.

There were always excessive police present—some of whom were discourteous and abrasive—whenever predominantly black groups gathered. But this time, if the police were there, they were not in sight and were doing nothing to calm the racist mob. The crowd grew and became very disruptive. People marched outside, and they broke into the meeting and continued their loud, offensive behavior. Young children who were in the group began to imitate the disorderly conduct of the adults. Dr. King had to discontinue his speech and was rushed out the back of the building.

We could not approach him. It was one of the largest displays of hate I have ever witnessed. We left as quickly as we could. It was difficult to get through the hostile crowd. I fell down on the ice and snow and broke the strap of my patent-leather purse. Fortunately, I was not badly hurt. Mr. Tappes assisted me to the car.

Dr. King was scheduled to return to Detroit on April 11, and I was sure I would have an opportunity to meet with him then, but he was assassinated on April 4.

The hurt I felt was almost unbearable when I heard of his death. It left me numb. It was almost as if I had been shot myself. His life and his leadership had meant so much to me that it is still difficult to describe what a personal loss it was.

I, along with many others, have accepted the challenge to fulfill his dream by fullfilling my own. The "beloved community" he often spoke of is one of respect and opportunity for all people.

# "You are as good as anyone"

Atlanta, Georgia, is today called the capital of the New South. It is a thriving, cosmopolitan city with a large middle-class African-American population, much of which moved to Atlanta from the North in search of a better life.

But back in the 1920s, Atlanta was heavily segregated; life was very hard even for the small black middle class. Most blacks who could manage it left Atlanta, lured by the promise of a better life in the North.

Martin Luther King, Jr., was born in Atlanta on January 15, 1929. His mother, Alberta Williams King, had deep roots in its small, black middle class. Her father, Adam Daniel Williams, had been pastor of Ebenezer Baptist Church for thirty-seven years. She herself was a schoolteacher, a highly respected profession in the black community and one of the few professions open to black women at that time.

Martin Luther King, Sr. (Martin's father), who was called Mike, had worked hard to become part of the middle class. Born on a farm some twenty miles outside Atlanta, he had determined to become something more than a farmer. Schooling for black children in the rural areas did not go past sixth grade, so to get more education Martin, Sr., went to Atlanta at the age of sixteen and worked in the freight yards by day while going to school at night. It took him eleven years to finish high school. After earning his high school diploma, he enrolled at Atlanta's black, all-male college, called Morehouse. Five years later he was ordained a Baptist minister.

Marrying Alberta Williams was a step up the social ladder for Martin, Sr. He moved into the comfortable Williams home on Auburn Avenue. His marriage also led first to the assistant pastorship of Ebenezer Baptist Church, and then to the pastorship, which he took over after his father-in-law died.

The first child born to Alberta and Martin King was a daughter, Christine. The following year Martin, Jr., was born. At first his parents gave him his father's nickname, and he was christened Michael. But shortly afterward the Kings decided he should have his father's real name, so he was renamed Martin Luther, Jr. Still, everyone called him Little Mike. The year following his birth, the Kings had another son. They named him for Mrs. King's father, who died the next year, but young Arthur Daniel was soon called simply "A.D."

The King children grew up in comfortable circumstances in a warm and loving household. Young Martin was especially close to his grandmother, whom the children called Mama Williams. He was twelve when she died in 1941, and he was so distraught that he jumped out of a second-floor window in the house. Fortunately he was not injured. It was not the first time he had jumped or fallen from that window because of something that had happened to his grandmother. Once, when their grandmother was still alive, and their parents were out of the house, A.D. had slid down a banister and knocked Mama Williams unconscious. Martin blamed himself for not watching his younger brother more carefully, and feeling responsible for his grandmother's injury, he went out the window.

With a father like Martin Luther King, Sr., a boy took his responsibilities seriously. The older man was very stern and did not spare the rod. But while his children learned to fear his anger, they never feared the man himself. Instead, the clear limits he set for them made them feel secure and loved.

Martin, Sr., believed his family should set an example for the rest of the congregation of Ebenezer Baptist Church. While his expectations placed a burden on his children, the young Kings also enjoyed the special distinction of being the

Martin's parents, Alberta and Martin Luther, Sr. "My mother, as the daughter of a successful minister, had grown up in comparative comfort....But my father, a sharecropper's son, had met [discrimination's] brutalities at first hand, and had begun to strike back at an early age."

Martin at a birthday party (bottom row, fourth from left).

minister's children. They took part in all the church activities and attended both Sunday school and regular services. Martin began singing in the choir at an early age.

The Bible was the most important book in their house, but there were many other books as well. Both the elder Kings constantly stressed the importance of education. For Martin King, Sr., education had been the way out of poverty. For the schoolteacher Alberta King it was equally important. She tutored all her children when they were very young, so that by the time they were old enough to start school they were far ahead of their classmates.

Young Martin was an especially quick learner, and Mrs. King felt he was ready to go to school when he was not yet five years old. There were no public preschool classes — not even kindergarten—and the school system did not accept youngsters until they were six. But Mrs. King was determined to get Martin into school. So in January 1934, just before his fifth birthday, she took him to Yonge Street School, the black school in their Auburn Avenue neighborhood, and enrolled him, saying he was six.

No one suspected that Martin was younger than his mother had said he was until that April, when Martin told his teacher about his last birthday party and the five candles on his cake. The teacher reported that he was underage, and Martin was promptly dismissed from the school. Reluctantly, Martin's mother waited until he was really six before she re-enrolled him. But by that time he was so advanced that he was soon skipped to the second grade.

Martin learned so fast that school was not a challenge for him. To keep him interested, his parents encouraged him to read the books in their large library. He did so, and he also frequently borrowed books from the colored branch of the Atlanta Public Library. But all those books were not enough. He wanted to buy them, too.

His parents could afford to buy the books Martin wanted, and they bought many for him. But his father decided it was time for Martin to start learning that he had to work for what he wanted. The elder King arranged a paper route for

Martin. With the money he earned delivering the *Atlanta Journal*, Martin bought books.

By this time Martin was learning another, much harder, lesson—how to live with dignity in the segregated world of Atlanta. While the King family was insulated from some of the worst racism by their small world of Auburn Avenue, the Ebenezer Baptist Church, and the neighborhood black school, there was no way to keep all of the ugliness out.

Martin was very young when he became aware of that ugliness. In his book *Stride Toward Freedom*, he recalled the first time he suffered discrimination.

While I was still too young for school I had already learned something about discrimination. For three or four years my inseparable playmates had been two white boys whose parents ran a store across the street from our home in Atlanta. Then something began to happen. When I went across the street to get them, their parents would say that they couldn't play. They weren't hostile; they just made excuses. Finally I asked my mother about it.

Every parent at some time faces the problem of explaining the facts of life to his child. Just as inevitably, for the Negro parent, the moment comes when he must explain to his offspring the facts of segregation. My mother took me on her lap and began by telling me about slavery and how it had ended with the Civil War. She tried to explain the divided system of the South—the segregated schools, restaurants, theaters, housing; the white and colored signs on drinking fountains, waiting rooms, lavatories—as a social condition rather than a natural order. Then she said the words that almost every Negro hears before he can yet understand the injustice that makes them necessary: "You are as good as anyone."

Even though Martin's parents taught him that it was his Christian duty to love everyone, for years afterward he hated white people. "As I grew older and older," he once said, "this feeling continued to grow."

Also as he grew older, Martin learned more about the injustice of racism. He heard adults talk about Jim Crow and finally realized that Jim Crow was not a person but a system of segregation. Jim Crow was the stage name of a white minstrel who performed in blackface makeup in the late 1800s. His act caricatured blacks. Somehow, the name Jim Crow came to stand for all the segregation laws that were instituted in the South after Union troops ended their occupation of the former Confederate States after the Civil War.

Martin learned in school that, as his mother had told him, blacks were descended from African slaves and that even though slavery had ended, whites continued to mistreat blacks. While his teachers also taught him about important black Americans who had succeeded despite the legacy of slavery, Martin knew that the teachers in his black school were not as well paid as those in the white schools, that his schoolbooks were castoffs from the white schools, that the sporting equipment and facilities at the black schools were not as good as those at the white schools, and that the black school buildings were not kept up as well as the white ones were.

Martin didn't just deliver the *Atlanta Journal*. He read it, too. Often the headlines were about lynchings, the illegal execution of blacks by white mobs such as the Ku Klux Klan, a group of vicious racial separatists. The articles urging people to vote in elections were aimed at whites, since most blacks were not allowed to vote. Many advertisements in the classified section warned "No Colored," meaning that black job seekers need not apply.

Martin wanted to know why whites treated blacks as if they were not as good as whites. His parents were hard-pressed to explain. It wasn't like answering the question, Why is the sky blue? The best they could do was agree that it was not fair and show by example that although they had to live with segregation, they did not have to bow to it.

Martin Luther King, Sr., was a proud man who had worked hard for his education and his position. He knew he had worked harder and knew more than many whites who thought themselves better than he. He often stood up to racist whites, making his wife fearful that he would one day get himself into trouble. In the South in those days a black man who stood up to whites could be in serious danger, as the frequent lynchings proved. But the Reverend King didn't do anything foolish; he simply refused to bow his head and suffer ill-treatment. His behavior had a lasting effect on his children.

Martin later described two such incidents with his father.

I remembered a trip to a downtown shoestore with Father when I was still small. We had sat down in the first empty seats at the front of the store. A young white clerk came up and murmured politely:

"I'll be happy to serve you if you'll just move to those seats in the rear."

My father answered, "There's nothing wrong with these seats. We're quite comfortable here."

"Sorry," said the clerk, "but you'll have to move."

"We'll either buy shoes sitting here," my father retorted, "or we won't buy shoes at all." Whereupon he took me by the hand and walked out of the store. This was the first time I had ever seen my father so angry. I still remember walking down the street beside him as he muttered, "I don't care how long I have to live with this system, I will never accept it."

And he never has. I remember riding with him another day when he accidentally drove past a stop sign. A policeman pulled up to the car and said:

"All right, boy, pull over and let me see your license."

My father replied indignantly, "I'm no boy." Then, pointing to me, "This is a boy. I'm a man, and until you call me one, I will not listen to you."

The policeman was so shocked that he wrote the ticket up nervously and left the scene as quickly as possible.

From before I was born, my father had refused to ride the city buses, after witnessing a brutal attack on a load of Negro passengers. He had led the fight in Atlanta to equalize teachers' salaries, and had been instrumental in the elimination of jim-crow elevators in the courthouse. As pastor of the Ebenezer Baptist Church, where he still presides over a congregation of four thousand, he had wielded great influence in the Negro community, and had perhaps won the grudging respect of the whites. At any rate, they had never attacked him physically, a fact that filled my brother and sister and me with wonder as we grew up in this tension-packed atmosphere.

Life was filled with tension for black people in Atlanta. They never knew when they might run into a racist white who didn't like the way they looked and tried to start trouble. They planned ahead carefully whenever they went downtown. They had to make sure they wouldn't be thirsty or have to use a bathroom because then they would have to search for a "Colored" water fountain or public restroom. And if they got hungry, they were in trouble, because they would not be served at most restaurants, except perhaps through the back door.

On the public buses blacks had to go up the front steps and pay and then go back down the steps and enter through the back door. They could sit down in the back rows if the bus was not full, but if it filled up and white people had to stand, then blacks had to give up even a seat in a back row to a white person.

Martin was about fourteen when he had his first confrontation on a public bus. He and his teacher, Miss Sarah Bradley, had traveled to an oratorical contest out of town. On their way

Martin's father preached in the Ebenezer Baptist Church. "With his fearless honesty and his robust, dynamic presence, his words commanded attention."

One day Martin would become the pastor of the Ebenezer Baptist Church, a block from his childhood home, where both his maternal grandfather and his father had been pastors before him.

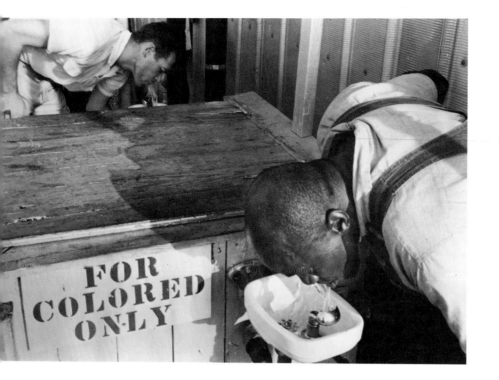

FOR COLORED ONLY

"Being a Negro in America is not a comfortable existence. It means being a part of the company of the bruised, the battered, the scarred, and the defeated....It means the ache and anguish of living in so many situations where hopes unborn have died."

Black people had to sit behind white people in the buses of the South. "As a teenager I had never been able to accept the fact of having to go to the back of a bus or sit in the segregated section of a train. The first time that I had been seated behind a curtain in a dining car, I felt as if the curtain had been dropped on my selfhood."

COLORED PASSENGERS

COLOR PASSENG

# "An inner urge"

Enrolling at Morehouse College at the age of fifteen was a fairly extraordinary accomplishment. But it did not take Martin long to realize that although he might have been brighter than his classmates in earlier years, his education in segregated schools had not prepared him for college work. He struggled through his four years at Morehouse.

He also struggled to decide what kind of career he wanted to pursue. He knew very well that nothing would please his parents more than for him to follow in his father's footsteps and enter the ministry. But Martin was skeptical about religion. It seemed to him that black religion, which was all he knew, concentrated too much on heaven and the rewards of the next life and not enough on the trials of this life. He also felt that religion appealed to the emotions more than to the intellect. Martin thought of majoring in law or medicine. He wasn't very good in science, so he dropped the idea of becoming a doctor. With a career in law in mind, he decided to major in sociology.

Although Martin lived at home and commuted by bus to Morehouse, he participated energetically in extracurricular activities. He was a member of the glee club and chorus and took part in oratorical contests. He also joined several interracial organizations that brought together black students from Morehouse and white students from Atlanta's white colleges.

Getting to know white students in these groups helped him overcome many of his anti-white feelings.

As he continued to think about his career choice, it occurred to Martin that two of the men at Morehouse whom he most admired were ministers. President Benjamin Mays and Professor George D. Kelsey were both learned men, and Martin realized he could be both a learned man and a minister. But what made him come to a final decision was his experience in the summer after his sophomore year, which he spent working in the tobacco fields outside Hartford, Connecticut. Martin and a group of friends made their first trip north to earn some extra money. The others chose Martin as their devotional leader, and he enjoyed the experience.

By early the following summer, Martin informed his parents that he wanted to enter the ministry. Almost immediately his father arranged for the board of deacons at Ebenezer Baptist Church to license him to preach. He was named assistant pastor.

That fall he started applying to seminaries. On his applications he gave as his reasons for wanting to be a minister "an inescapable urge to serve society" and "a sense of responsibility which I could not escape." A few years later, he would elaborate on his reasons.

> I had felt the urge to enter the ministry from my latter high school days, but accumulated doubts had somewhat blocked the urge. Now it appeared again with an inescapable drive. My call to the ministry was not a miraculous or supernatural something; on the contrary, it was an inner urge calling me to save humanity. I guess the influence of my father also had a great deal to do with my going into the ministry. This is not to say that he ever spoke to me in terms of being a minister, but that my admiration for him was the great moving factor. He set forth a noble example that I didn't mind following.

Martin was accepted at Crozer Theological Seminary in Chester, Pennsylvania. He found himself in a largely white student body for the first time. Of the fewer than one hundred students, only a handful were black. But by this time he had come to understand that all white people were not racist. He developed close friendships with two white students as well as with an older black classmate. "Little Mike," as Martin continued to be known at Crozer, enjoyed his first experience of being away from home for an extended period of time. He became involved in a myriad of social activities, and eventually he was elected president of the student body.

He also worked hard at his studies. Every year his grades got better until in his senior year he got straight As. Intellectually, he seemed to have made the right career choice. He understood the concepts of religion and became a very good debater. He was especially interested in the theories of religious intellectuals who held that the power of Christian love could be used to advance social justice. He was looking for a new way to apply philosophical and religious concepts to the plight of southern black people—a way that would take the emphasis off waiting for the rewards in heaven and place it on gaining the rights and dignity enjoyed by other people during earthly life.

Thus he was very interested in the ideas of the nineteenth-century poet and essayist Henry David Thoreau, who believed in civil disobedience as a way to oppose unjust laws, and of A. J. Muste, a twentieth-century Catholic priest and pacifist who was against using any form of violence to solve disputes. And when Martin chanced to hear a lecture about a man in India named Mohandas K. Gandhi, who was using the principles of nonviolence to bring about tremendous social change, he was truly inspired.

Born in India in 1869 to an upper class, Gandhi realized that the British kept control over India by pitting the different classes of its rigid caste system against one another as well as by inflaming long-standing controversies between Indian Hindus and Indian Muslims. His call for independence from Britain included a plea to the upper classes, which traditionally exploited the lower classes as manual laborers, to

Martin (front row, left) attends a lecture at Morehouse College at the age of nineteen.

Martin discovered the nonviolent teachings of Mahatma Gandhi at the Crozer Theological Seminary. "You ought to believe something in life—believe that thing so fervently that you will stand up with it till the end of your days. I can't make myself believe that God wants me to hate. I'm tired of violence....We have a power ...as old as the insights of Jesus of Nazareth and as modern as the techniques of Mahatma Gandhi."

become more self-reliant. He urged Hindus and Muslims to put aside their differences and unite in the cause of independence. He also called on all Indians to resist the British through noncooperation and nonviolent protest.

Gandhi, who came to be called "Mahatma," or Great Soul, then began to disobey various British laws. He was arrested and jailed but did not try to defend himself. Against the might of the British authorities he had only his *satyagraha*, or "soul force." Soon other Indians began to follow his example by resisting unfair laws, boycotting British goods, and refusing to bow to class customs and religious separatism. Scores were arrested; they filled the jails to overflowing. But this served only to attract more Indians to the cause of independence from Britain. It took seventeen long years, but Gandhi's "soul force" and the unity of the Indian people against British rule, coupled with world opinion—which eventually sided with Gandhi—caused Britain at last to surrender India to the Indians.

The idea of bringing about such revolutionary change through nonviolence excited Martin. But he could not imagine how the concept of nonviolent protest could be applied to segregation in the American South. White racists were so determined to keep black people down by any means necessary that Martin didn't believe anything short of armed rebellion could bring about equality for southern blacks.

Martin thrived on his religious studies. But he had much to learn about preaching, especially to black congregations. Students at Crozer were assigned student pastorships in which they would preach at churches on the East Coast twice a month. Martin was assigned to the First Baptist Church in Queens, New York. The pastor at that church felt that Martin was something of a snob and too aloof and unemotional to give a successful sermon to his black congregation. Yet in 1950, Martin Luther King, Jr., had no hope of becoming pastor to anything but a black church.

When Martin graduated from Crozer, his family expected him to come home and take up his duties as assistant pastor of Ebenezer Baptist Church. But Martin wanted to continue his studies. He applied to Boston University and was accepted into its doctoral program in theology. There was so much more to know, he explained to his parents. They accepted his wishes and were pleased with his ambition. His father even gave him a brand-new green Chevrolet for his trip to Boston.

In Boston, Martin not only studied but enjoyed an active social life as well. He soon found, however, that he was more comfortable with women who were from the South than with northern women. Thus he was pleased to be introduced to Coretta Scott, who was studying performing arts at the New England Conservatory of Music in Boston. The pretty Coretta was from the small town of Heiberger, Alabama, and she was a serious, ambitious young woman. Martin fell in love with her immediately.

Coretta cared deeply for Martin, too, but she was not sure if his dreams for the future would mesh with her dreams. He planned to return to the South to take up a pastorship; she wanted to stay in the North. He wanted a proper minister's wife, and she wanted to have a career as a singer. But Martin, with years of debating experience behind him, could be very persuasive. Coretta accepted his proposal of marriage, and they were wed on June 18, 1953, on her father's lawn in Heiberger. The ceremony was performed by the Reverend King, Sr.

Martin and Coretta King returned to Boston and their studies. Martin was not finished with his doctoral work, but already he was getting offers from churches to be their pastor. He turned down offers from two northern churches, one in Boston and one in New York. When the elders of Dexter Avenue Baptist Church in Montgomery, Alabama, wrote to say that their church was without a pastor, Martin agreed to be a guest preacher there one Sunday in January 1954.

Dexter Avenue Baptist Church was a small, red-brick building with white doors and steeple and well-kept grounds. It was within sight of the white state government buildings, including the state capitol, where the Confederate flag continued to fly in proud memory of a lost era. But this location did not make Martin feel especially uncomfortable. He had grown

Coretta Scott was studying to be a singer when she met Martin in Boston. They were married on June 18, 1953.

After completing his doctoral work in theology at Boston University, King was eager to begin preaching. "Whatever your life's work is, do it well."

The Dexter Avenue
Baptist Church in
Montgomery, Alabama,
where King accepted
his first pastorship.

up in segregation and believed he could live with it if he followed the example of his father.

Inside, the church was gleaming polished wood, and when the sun shone through the stained-glass windows, it was beautiful. Martin liked the church immediately and started thinking how nice it would be to have a church like that. He had worked hard on his sermon, which was very well received. Soon a formal invitation arrived asking him to be pastor of the church. Martin and Coretta talked it over. Martin wanted his own church and did not want to be assistant pastor to his father. Coretta still preferred the North, but she decided that at least Montgomery was a large enough city to offer her a chance to perform concerts there. King remembered their lengthy discussion.

For several days we talked and thought and prayed over each of these matters. Finally we agreed that, in spite of the disadvantages and inevitable sacrifices, our greatest service could be rendered in our native South. We came to the conclusion that we had something of a moral obligation to return—at least for a few years.

The South, after all, was our home. Despite its shortcomings we loved it as home, and had a real desire to do something about the problems that we had felt so keenly as youngsters. We never wanted to be considered detached spectators. Since racial discrimination was most intense in the South, we felt that some of the Negroes who had received a portion of their training in other sections of the country should return to share their broader contacts and educational experience in its solution. Moreover, despite having to sacrifice much of the cultural life we loved, despite the existence of Jim Crow which kept reminding us at all times of the color of our skin, we had the feeling that something remarkable was unfolding in the South, and we wanted to be on hand to witness it.

Martin, with his wife Coretta and their baby, Yolanda, greets church members on the steps of the Dexter Avenue Church. The state capitol dome looms in the background. "Love is somehow the key that unlocks the door which leads to ultimate reality."

Martin wrote back that he accepted the pastorship. He and Coretta could be in Montgomery in September.

Just a few months later, in May 1954, the United States Supreme Court ruled in the case of *Brown v. Topeka Board of Education* that segregated public schools were unconstitutional. The case against "separate but equal" schools had been pursued all the way to the highest court in the land by the National Association for the Advancement of Colored People (NAACP), an interracial organization founded in the early years of the twentieth century. The NAACP had been fighting long and hard against segregated schools, and the Supreme Court ruling was a great victory, even though the Court stopped short of giving a timetable for segregated public schools to integrate. Instead, the Court said segregation should be ended with "all deliberate speed." Many people hoped the decision would drive a wedge into the wall of segregation running through other areas of life in the South. Martin and Coretta King were certainly hopeful that they would be returning to a South on the verge of change.

In September 1954, Martin and Coretta moved into the old, seven-room white frame parsonage of Dexter Avenue Baptist Church in the middle of Montgomery's black middle-class neighborhood. Feeling settled at last, they soon started a family. Their daughter Yolanda Denise was born in November 1955. They called her Yoki.

However, by the time Yoki was born the Kings were having second thoughts about spending the rest of their lives in Montgomery. Segregation controlled the lives of Montgomery blacks in every possible area, and the whites were determined to keep it that way. Martin and Coretta had been warned from the start not to challenge the system of discrimination and segregation, and Martin soon understood why. Every minor step blacks took toward dignity was answered with an iron fist. Martin began to wish that he had returned to Atlanta, where his brother, A.D., had become a minister and settled. Compared with Montgomery, Atlanta was downright liberal. Still, he thought that there were things he could do to better the lives of his parishioners. He had no idea that very soon he would be called on to lead a tidal wave of change.

**King accepts the presidency of the Montgomery Improvement Association, the group that led the year-long boycott of the city's segregated bus system to its successful conclusion.**

# MONTGOMERY

# "My feet is real tired, but my soul is rested"

On Thursday, December 1, 1955, Mrs. Rosa Parks left her job at Montgomery Fair Department Store and boarded the Cleveland Avenue bus for home. She took a seat in the middle section of the bus, in the front row of the "Colored section." At the next stop, several white passengers boarded. They filled up the white seats, and one man was left standing. The driver looked back and noticed the man. Then he looked back at Mrs. Parks and the other black people sitting in the same row and said, "Let me have those front seats."

The others in the row stood up. Rosa Parks refused to do so. She had obeyed the segregation laws for all her forty-two years, but she was suddenly tired of giving in. She was arrested and charged with violating the segregation ordinance.

This was not the first time a black woman had been arrested for refusing to give up her seat. But now, for the first time, blacks in Montgomery decided to do something about it. In protest, they boycotted the city buses the following Monday. Local black leaders were amazed at this show of courage by people who had bowed to segregation for so many years. They decided to continue the protest for a week. The group met and decided to elect the Reverend Martin Luther King, Jr., as its president. They then came up with a name for their organization: They called themselves the Montgomery Improvement Association (MIA).

The group did not know King well. But what they did know was that King was so new in town that he'd not had a chance to make any strong friends or enemies. He had not accepted favors from the whites of Montgomery and so did not owe them anything.

King was astonished to be elected. He had just finished his doctoral thesis and had planned to devote all his time to his congregation. But he did not feel that he could decline. Besides, he was excited about the possibilities for nonviolent protest that the boycott presented. All his thoughts about how Gandhi had led the Indian people to independence through nonviolent protest came back to him now. He hadn't believed it was possible to apply those principles to the fight against segregation in the southern United States. But the black people of Montgomery had surprised him with their one-day boycott. Maybe it could happen here after all. He realized that if the boycott was to continue and be successful, blacks would have to swallow their terror and press on, for he knew the whites of Montgomery would use any means necessary to stop the protest. He himself swallowed hard when he thought about the great responsibility that had been thrust upon him. As president of the new organization, he had to speak at a mass meeting that had been called at the Holt Street Baptist Church.

King later recalled that for the first time in his life he had to speak without preparation.

Without manuscript or notes, I told the story of what had happened to Mrs. Parks. Then I reviewed the long history of abuses and insults that Negro citizens had experienced on the city buses. "But there comes a time," I said, "that people get tired. We are here this evening to say to those who have mistreated us so long that we are tired— tired of being segregated and humiliated; tired of being kicked about by the brutal feet of oppression." The congregation met this statement with fervent applause. "We had no alternative but to protest," I continued. "For many years, we have shown amazing patience. We have sometimes given our white brothers the feeling that we liked the way we were being treated. But we come here tonight to be saved from that patience that makes us patient with anything less than freedom and justice." Again the audience interrupted with applause.

Briefly I justified our actions, both morally and legally. "One of the great glories of democracy is the right to protest for right." Comparing our methods with those of the white citizens councils and the Ku Klux Klan, I pointed out that while "these organizations are protesting for the perpetuation of injustice in the community, we are protesting for the birth of justice in the community. Their methods lead to violence and lawlessness. But in our protest there will be no cross burnings. No white person will be taken from his home by a hooded Negro mob and brutally murdered. There will be no threats and intimidation. We will be guided by the highest principle of law and order."

With this groundwork for militant action, I moved on to words of caution. I urged the people not to force anybody to refrain from riding the buses. "Our method will be that of persuasion, not coercion. We will only say to the people, 'Let your conscience be your guide.' " Emphasizing the Christian doctrine of love, "our actions must be guided by the deepest principles of our Christian faith. Love must be our regulating ideal. Once again we must hear the words of Jesus echoing across the centuries: 'Love your enemies, bless them that curse you, and pray for them that despitefully use you.' If we fail to do this our protest will end up as a meaningless drama on the stage of history, and its memory will be shrouded with the ugly garments of shame. In spite of the mistreatment that we have confronted we must not become bitter, and end up hating our white brothers. As Booker T. Washington said, 'Let no man pull you so low as to make you hate him.' " Once more the audience responded enthusiastically.

Then came my closing statement. "If you will protest courageously, and yet with dignity and Christian love, when the history books are written in future generations, the historians will have to pause and say, 'There lived a great people—a black people—who injected new meaning and dignity into the veins of civilization.' This is our challenge and our overwhelming responsibility." As I took my seat the people rose to their feet and applauded. I was thankful to God that the message had gotten over and that the task of combining the militant and the moderate had been at least partially accomplished. The people had been as enthusiastic when I urged them to love as they were when I urged them to protest.

As I sat listening to the continued applause I realized that this speech had evoked more response than any speech or sermon I had ever delivered, and yet it was virtually unprepared. I came to see for the first time what the older preachers meant when they said, "Open your mouth and God will speak for you." While I would not let this experience tempt me to overlook the need for continued preparation, it would always remind me that God can transform man's weakness into his glorious opportunity.

In that one unprepared speech the young Reverend Martin Luther King, Jr., brought to bear not just his innermost feelings but also the things he had learned studying philosophy, especially the principles of nonviolence that Mohandas Gandhi had lived by. And in that one speech Martin Luther King, Jr., set the tone for the nonviolent, direct-action civil rights movement that would change America.

Fired up by King's speech, and by their own determination not to be humiliated any longer on the city's buses, the black people of Montgomery continued the boycott. Those

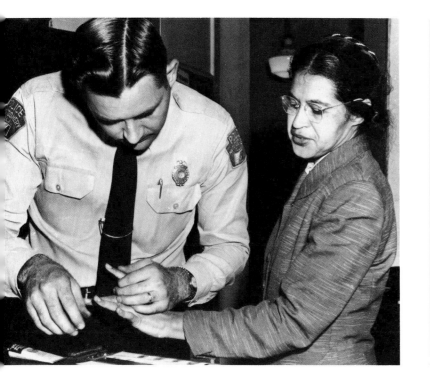

Rosa Parks is finger-
printed upon her arrest
for refusing to give up
her seat to a white
man on a city bus.
"Mrs. Parks's refusal
to move back was her
intrepid affirmation
that she had had
enough. It was an
individual expression
of a timeless longing
for human dignity
and freedom."

During the bus boy-
cott, carpools were
a common sight.

who could walk to work did so. Those who had too far to go took taxis. Black taxi drivers transported black riders for the same fare as the buses charged. When the city of Montgomery refused to permit the taxi drivers to charge such low fares, people organized car pools.

Meanwhile, media coverage of the boycott spurred sympathy in many other parts of the country, and contributions to the MIA poured in. The MIA bought vans to be operated by the various black churches and set up a system to match the vans with riders.

While some white employers fired their black workers who took part in the boycott, some white women indirectly aided the boycott by driving their maids and babysitters to and from work. Many white men got angry about this, but the women refused to stop.

Since the great majority of bus riders were blacks, the Montgomery city-bus system could not afford to run for long without them. It was the first time that blacks in the city had demonstrated the economic power of their sheer numbers. Now, white racists became even more determined to stop the boycott. Membership in local chapters of the Ku Klux Klan and the White Citizens Council, another white supremacist group, increased. Members of the Montgomery Improvement Association had been receiving threatening telephone calls from the beginning. On Monday, January 30, 1956, someone carried through on a threat: The King home was bombed. Coretta was at home with Yolanda, but fortunately they were not hurt. The homes of other black ministers were also bombed as the boycott continued and white resistance mounted.

Martin Luther King and the other leaders of the MIA constantly held meetings to remind the black community that they must not react to violence with violence. Even though the boycott had dragged on and on, the tired black people of Montgomery refused to fight back. Several years later, King would recall that the boycotters had come to feel an inner peace about the rightness of what they were doing.

A White Citizens Council rallied against the boycott.

King calmed an angry crowd from the porch steps of his home just after the house had been bombed. "We must not return violence under any condition. I know this is difficult advice to follow, especially since we have been the victims of no less than ten bombings. But this is the way of Christ; it is the way of the cross. We must somehow believe that unearned suffering is redemptive."

On a chill morning in the autumn of 1956, an elderly, toilworn Negro woman in Montgomery, Alabama, began her slow, painful, four-mile walk to her job. It was the tenth month of the Montgomery bus boycott, which had begun with a life expectancy of one week. The old woman's difficult progress led a passerby to inquire sympathetically if her feet were tired. Her simple answer became the boycotter's watchword. "Yes, friend, my feet is real tired, but my soul is rested."

The more white violence broke out, and the more black non-violence was maintained, the greater was the television coverage of the boycott, and the more national attention and sympathy were aroused. Contributions continued to pour in. The MIA used some of the money to pay attorneys, for the city of Montgomery and the state of Alabama tried many legal means to stop the boycott, including arresting King and others in the MIA for violating a state ordinance that prohibited boycotts.

The matter of discrimination on Montgomery's buses and of the boycott went from the local courts to the federal district court and finally all the way to the United States Supreme Court. On November 13, 1956, the Supreme Court declared segregation on Montgomery's buses unconstitutional. But although the decision was announced, the official decree would not be served on the city and the state for another month. The Montgomery Improvement Association decided not to end the boycott until that time. Finally, a few days before Christmas, 1956, the official decree was served and the long boycott ended.

Martin Luther King's joy was tempered by the awareness that whites would not take the official decree lying down. After blacks returned to the buses, bricks were thrown through bus windows. Black women were slapped, black men

**King was arrested for violating a state law prohibiting boycotts.**

**Ralph Abernathy,
King's close friend
and associate (left),
congratulated King
when the Supreme
Court finally ruled
that Alabama's
segregation laws
on buses were
unconstitutional.**

**King rides the
first integrated bus
In Montgomery.**

Since few southern blacks were able to read or write, the literacy test was a way to effectively deny them the vote. "We can never be satisfied as long as a Negro in Mississippi cannot vote and a Negro in New York believes he has nothing for which to vote."

King's address at the Prayer Pilgrimage for Freedom in Washington, D.C., brought him national recognition.

my mind—it is made up for me. I cannot live as a demo-cratic citizen, observing the laws I have helped to enact—I can only submit to the edict of others.

So our most urgent request to the president of the United States and every member of Congress is to give us the right to vote.

Give us the ballot and we will no longer have to worry the federal government about our basic rights.

Give us the ballot and we will no longer plead to the federal government for passage of an antilynching law; we will by the power of our vote write the law on the statute books of the southern states and bring an end to the dastardly acts of the hooded perpetrators of violence.

Give us the ballot and we will transform the salient misdeeds of blood-thirsty mobs into the calculated good deeds of orderly citizens.

Give us the ballot and we will fill our legislative halls with men of good will. . . .

Give us the ballot and we will place judges on the benches of the South who will "do justly and love mercy," and we will place at the head of the southern states gover-nors who have felt not only the tang of the human, but the glow of the divine.

Give us the ballot and we will quietly and nonvio-lently, without rancor or bitterness, implement the Su-preme Court's decision of May 17, 1954.

But while King's speech was a stirring one, and the first of many inspirational speeches and rallies in the voting rights cause, the SCLC could not attract the support for its issue that the Montgomery bus boycott had enjoyed. Something was missing. The commitment, the energy, the sense of unity and driving purpose just weren't there. King realized that it would take more of his time than he had expected to inspire south-ern blacks to support the voting rights issue.

In addition, a near tragedy occurred that caused King to think seriously about what he wanted to do with his life, for it made him realize that he might not have many years in which to do it.

His first book, *Stride Toward Freedom*, was published in the late summer of 1958. To promote the book, he went to Blumstein's department store in Harlem, New York City, to autograph copies. There a deranged woman stabbed him with a letter opener. After her arrest, Mrs. Izola Curry charged that King was a communist. She also said she thought he was the head of the NAACP. She was later committed to a state hospital for the criminally insane.

King's brush with death caused some people, including King himself, to compare him to Gandhi, who had been assassinated by a Hindu religious fanatic. King had long dreamed of going to India to see for himself what Gandhi had accomplished, and he decided to make the trip. In February and March 1959, he and Coretta and Lawrence D. Reddick, a professor of history at the black Alabama State College in Montgomery, traveled in that land. King wrote about his impressions in an article for *Ebony* magazine.

The trip had a great impact on me personally. It was wonderful to be in Gandhi's land, to talk with his son, his grandsons, his cousins and other relatives; to share the reminiscences of his close comrades, to visit his ashrama to see the countless memorials for him and finally to lay a wreath on his entombed ashes at Rajghat. I left India more convinced than ever before that nonviolent resistance is the most potent weapon available to oppressed people in their struggle for freedom. It was a marvelous thing to see the amazing results of a nonviolent campaign. The aftermath of hatred and bitterness that usually follows a violent campaign was nowhere found in India. Today a mutual friendship based on complete equality exists between the Indian and British people

King was stabbed by a deranged woman in a Harlem department store while autographing copies of *Stride Toward Freedom*. "[The surgeon] told me that the razor tip of the instrument had been touching my aorta and that my whole chest had to be opened to extract it...the knife of violence was just that close to the nation's aorta."

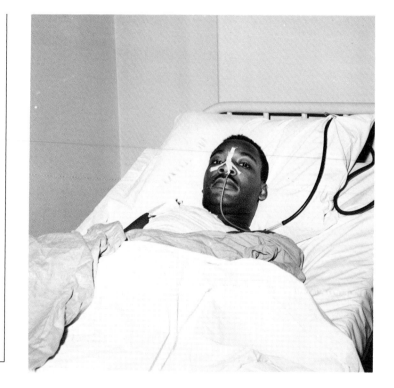

Mahatma Gandhi's nonviolent teachings were King's lifelong inspiration. "If humanity is to progress, Gandhi is inescapable. He lived, thought, and acted, inspired by the vision of humanity evolving toward a world of peace and harmony. We may ignore him at our own risk."

serve as its adviser. He participated in some of the sit-ins and was arrested and jailed.

In April 1961, one year after the birth of SNCC, members of that organization met with members of the SCLC and CORE to discuss future actions in the South. It was decided that the next target for desegregation would be interstate buses in the South. King was named chairman of the committee formed to coordinate these actions, which came to be called Freedom Rides.

On the Freedom Rides, integrated groups of civil rights workers boarded interstate buses in Washington, D.C., and traveled through the South. At preplanned stops, they disembarked and attempted to desegregate bus-station dining and restroom facilities. No serious trouble occurred at the first few stops, but as the buses went farther south, white resistance became violent. Crowds of whites beat up the Freedom Riders in Rock Hill, South Carolina, and Anniston, Alabama. But the Freedom Rides continued. By this time U.S. Attorney General Robert F. Kennedy had sent federal troops to the South to escort the buses, to protect them and their riders from further violence.

King despaired. This was not the kind of movement he had envisioned. He did not see much progress if four hundred federal troops had to protect a handful of bus riders. Moreover, only a small number of people participated in the Freedom Rides. Gradually the SCLC and CORE withdrew their support for the Freedom Rides, and SNCC continued them alone until, on September 22, 1961, the Interstate Commerce Commission ruled against segregation on all interstate vehicles and public facilities.

While King was pleased with that victory, he did not like the way it had been won. The tone of the civil rights movement was changing. The tactics of confrontation being employed by SNCC and other young militants were a grave departure from the nonviolent principles he believed in. But he had to admit they were effective. He and others in the SCLC felt they had to regain control of the civil rights movement and decided to adopt publicly the tone of confrontation while working behind the scenes to negotiate with authorities.

**Reverend King and Reverend Ralph Abernathy lead a protest march in Birmingham on April 12, 1963.**

# BIRMINGHAM

# "Now is the time"

King and others in the SCLC decided to launch a massive, general campaign for civil rights in Albany, Georgia. But the campaign soon went awry because there was not enough coordination among the various civil rights groups operating there. King learned the lesson of organization in Albany and applied it to the next campaign in Birmingham.

Birmingham was generally regarded as Alabama's most segregated big city. In fact, seventeen bombings of black churches in the city between 1957 and 1962 had earned the city the nickname "Bombingham." The members of the SCLC planned the campaign for April 1963 and informed the Kennedy administration in Washington, D.C., although they hoped they would not need the aid of federal troops. They also informed the city authorities, prompting a group of eight white Alabama clergymen to issue a public "Appeal for Law and Order" that called for meetings among prominent blacks and whites and stressed that obedience to the rulings of federal and local courts would solve Birmingham's racial problems. It also called the actions that King and the SCLC were planning "unwise and untimely."

King smarted from the criticism and especially resented the fact that it came from clergymen. But he was too busy to take the time to reply to the "Appeal." Although he did return to Atlanta in time to see his daughter Bernice Albertine born, by the next day he was back in Birmingham.

At meetings there, King urged all demonstrators to refrain from violence and reminded them that the goal of desegregation was a reconciliation with whites and not a victory over them. Many signed a pledge to go to prison, for King hoped to pack the Birmingham jails, just as Gandhi and his followers had packed the jails in India.

The campaign began peacefully with student sit-ins at a few lunch counters. There were many arrests and jailings, but there was no violence. Many blacks in Birmingham who had been afraid of violence now joined the campaign, and as it grew, the city authorities became worried. On Good Friday, King himself was arrested and jailed. He hoped that by going to jail himself he would encourage other black ministers, noticeably absent from the campaign, to join. But they did not.

In a way, King was glad to be in jail at that moment, for he finally had the time to respond to the criticism of his ideas and work that was contained in the "Appeal for Law and Order." Writing first in the margins of a newspaper brought to him by one of his aides, the Reverend Andrew Young, and then on scraps of paper supplied by a black prison trusty, he composed his answer, which was nineteen pages long when transcribed. "Letter from Birmingham City Jail" was destined to become one of the most famous essays on human rights ever written. Here is part of this historic letter:

April 16, 1963

My dear Fellow Clergymen:
While confined here in the Birmingham city jail, I came across your recent statements calling my present activities "unwise and untimely." Seldom do I pause to answer criticism of my work and ideas . . . I would have no time for constructive work. But since I feel that you are men of genuine good will and that your criticisms are sincerely

set forth, I want to try to answer your statements in what I hope will be patient and reasonable terms.

I think I should indicate why I am here in Birmingham, since you have been influenced by the view which argues against "outsiders coming in." I have the honor of serving as president of the Southern Christian Leadership Conference, an organization operating in every southern state, with headquarters in Atlanta, Georgia. . . . Several months ago the affiliate here in Birmingham asked us to be on call to engage in a nonviolent direct action program if such were deemed necessary. We readily consented, and when the hour came we lived up to our promise. . . .

But more basically, I am in Birmingham because injustice is here. . . .

You may well ask: "Why direct action? Why sit-ins, marches and so forth? Isn't negotiation a better path?" You are quite right in calling for negotiation. Indeed, this is the very purpose of direct action. Nonviolent direct action seeks to create such a crisis and foster such a tension that a community which has constantly refused to negotiate is forced to confront the issue. It seeks so to dramatize the issue that it can no longer be ignored. My citing the creation of tension as part of the work of the nonviolent-register may sound shocking. But I confess that I am not afraid of the word "tension." I have earnestly opposed violent tension, but there is a type of constructive, nonviolent tension which is necessary for growth . . . we must see the need for nonviolent gadflies to create the kind of tension in society that will help men rise from the dark depths of prejudice and racism to the majestic heights of understanding and brotherhood.

The purpose of our direct-action program is to create a situation so crisis-packed that it will inevitably open the door to negotiation. I therefore concur with you in your call for negotiation. Too long has our beloved South-

five-year-old son who is asking: "Daddy, why do white people treat colored people so mean?"; when you take a cross-country drive and find it necessary to sleep night after night in the uncomfortable corners of your automobile because no motel will accept you; when you are humiliated day in and day out by nagging signs reading "white" and "colored"; when your first name becomes "nigger," your middle name becomes "boy" (however old you are) and your last name becomes "John"; and your wife and mother are never given the respected title "Mrs."; when you are harried by day and haunted by night by the fact that you are a Negro, living constantly at tiptoe stance, never quite knowing what to expect next, and are plagued with inner fears and outer resentments; when you are forever fighting a degenerating sense of "nobodiness"—then you will understand why we find it difficult to wait. There comes a time when the cup of endurance runs over, and men are no longer willing to be plunged into the abyss of despair. I hope, sirs, you can understand our legitimate and unavoidable impatience.

You express a great deal of anxiety over our willingness to break laws. This is certainly a legitimate concern. Since we so diligently urge people to obey the Supreme Court's decision of 1954 outlawing segregation in public schools, at first glance it may seem rather paradoxical for us to consciously break laws. One may well ask: "How can you advocate breaking some laws and obeying others?" The answer lies in the fact that there are two types of laws: just and unjust. I would be the first to advocate obeying just laws. One has not only a legal but a moral responsibility to obey just laws. Conversely, one has a moral responsibility to disobey unjust laws. I would agree with St. Augustine that "an unjust law is no law at all." . . .

I must make two honest confessions to you, my Christian and Jewish brothers. First, I must confess that over the past few years I have been gravely disappointed with the white moderate. I have almost reached the regrettable conclusion that the Negro's great stumbling block in his stride toward freedom is not the White Citizens' Counciler or the Ku Klux Klanner, but the white moderate, who is more devoted to "order" than to justice; who prefers a negative peace which is the absence of tension to a positive peace which is the presence of justice; who constantly says: "I agree with you in the goal you seek, but I cannot agree with your methods of direct action"; who paternalistically believes he can set the timetable for another man's freedom; who lives by a mythical concept of time and who constantly advises the Negro to wait for a "more convenient season." Shallow understanding from people of good will is more frustrating than absolute misunderstanding from people of ill will. Lukewarm acceptance is much more bewildering than outright rejection. . . .

I had also hoped that the white moderate would reject the myth concerning time in relation to the struggle for freedom. I have just received a letter from a white brother in Texas. He writes: "All Christians know that the colored people will receive equal rights eventually, but it is possible that you are in too great a religious hurry. It has taken Christianity almost two thousand years to accomplish what it has. The teachings of Christ take a long time to come to earth." Such an attitude stems from a tragic misconception of time, from the strangely irrational notion that there is something in the very flow of time that will inevitably cure all ills. Actually, time itself is neutral; it can be used either destructively or constructively. More and more I feel that the people of ill will have used time much more effectively than have the people of good will. We will have to repent in this generation not merely for the hateful words and actions of the bad people but the appalling silence of the good people. Human progress never rolls in on wheels of inevitability; it comes through the tireless efforts of men willing to be co-workers with

God, and without this hard work, time itself becomes an ally of the forces of social stagnation. We must use time creatively, in the knowledge that the time is always ripe to do right. Now is the time to make real the promise of democracy and transform our pending national elegy into a creative psalm of brotherhood. Now is the time to lift our national policy from the quicksand of racial injustice to the solid rock of human dignity. . . .

Never before have I written such a long letter. I'm afraid it is much too long to take your precious time. I can assure you that it would have been much shorter if I had been writing from a comfortable desk, but what else can one do when he is alone in a narrow jail cell, other than write long letters, think long thoughts and pray long prayers?

If I have said anything in this letter that overstates the truth and indicates an unreasonable impatience, I beg you to forgive me. If I have said anything that understates the truth and indicates my having a patience that allows me to settle for anything less than brotherhood, I beg God to forgive me. . . .

Yours for the cause of Peace and Brotherhood,
Martin Luther King, Jr.

---

King was in prison for eight days. When he was released, he learned that a new tactic was being planned for the Birmingham campaign. The black children of the city were organizing at the Sixteenth Street Baptist Church to desegregate public libraries and parks. But Birmingham Sheriff Eugene "Bull" Connor had had enough. His men set on the children with snarling, snapping dogs. City firemen went after them with their powerful fire hoses, shooting streams of water that slammed them against buildings and sent them flying in all directions.

**Right:** Birmingham schoolchildren were arrested for joining in a civil rights demonstration.

**Below left:** Sheriff Eugene "Bull" Connor had had enough.

**Below right:** Firemen turn high-pressure hoses on peaceful demonstrators.

**Facing page:** On May 2, 1963, police dogs were used to attack demonstrators.

As police
violence
and arrests
increased,
so too did
the numbers
of blacks
who marched
in protest.

Birmingham's black adults responded to these acts of brutality against the children with so many marches and demonstrations that the white business leaders of the city called for negotiations. King and other SCLC leaders met with a group of these businessmen and announced in early May 1963 a plan to desegregate stores, provide more jobs for blacks, and set up biracial committees to look into grievances and solve future problems.

This was not the kind of campaign that King had hoped for, but once again the tactics of confrontation had succeeded. It was time, decided the leaders of the major civil rights organizations, to take the campaign to Washington, D.C., in a massive March on Washington to demand a strong civil rights bill.

On August 28, 1963, King and other civil rights leaders headed
the March on Washington for Jobs and Freedom.

# "Fire hoses, snarling dogs, and even death"

Actually, the March on Washington had been planned for some time. Originally the idea of A. Philip Randolph—president of the first black union, the Brotherhood of Sleeping Car Porters—the march brought together the leaders of all five major civil rights organizations in a concerted action for the first time. The idea behind the march was to take the case for a strong civil rights bill directly to Congress and the president.

President John F. Kennedy did not want to be put in a position of publicly bowing to pressure exerted by the marchers. On June 11 he appeared on national television and called for the country to fulfill its promise of freedom and equality and for Congress to pass an effective civil rights bill. It was the strongest commitment to civil rights ever voiced publicly by an American president.

The March on Washington on August 28, 1963, was the largest and most peaceful demonstration that had ever occurred in the nation's capital. It was a celebration of the progress made so far and the promise of progress to come. Some 250,000 people participated from all over the country, and between 60,000 and 95,000 of them were whites. Organized down to the smallest detail by Bayard Rustin, A. Philip Randolph's assistant, the march went off without a hitch. A quarter of a million people were moved in and out of the capital in a single day, fed, provided with sanitary facilities, and treated to an experience they would remember for the rest of their lives.

The highlight of the day came with the ceremonies on the steps of the Lincoln Memorial. Well-known black singers performed, and the leaders of all the civil rights organizations gave speeches. King spoke last because by this time he had a reputation for eloquence, and no one wanted to follow him. They were right not to, for King's speech that day is his best remembered.

He had prepared a rather solemn speech that dwelt on the injustices suffered by blacks for three hundred years. But by the time he was scheduled to give the keynote speech, the joy of the day had infected him. The march was a real demonstration of what he envisioned America could be. After finishing his prepared speech, he shared his dream with the nation.

So I say to you, my friends, that even though we must face the difficulties of today and tomorrow, I still have a dream. It is a dream deeply rooted in the American dream that one day this nation will rise up and live out the true meaning of its creed—we hold these truths to be self-evident, that all men are created equal.

I have a dream that one day on the red hills of Georgia, sons of former slaves and sons of former slave-owners will be able to sit down together at the table of brotherhood.

I have a dream that one day, even the state of Mississippi, a state sweltering in the heat of injustice, sweltering with the heat of oppression, will be transformed into an oasis of freedom and justice.

I have a dream my four little children will one day live in a nation where they will not be judged by the color of their skin but by the content of their character. I have a dream today!

**King delivers his "I have a dream" speech at the Lincoln Memorial.**

A quarter of a million people came together in peace.

I have a dream that one day, down in Alabama, with its vicious racists . . . little black boys and black girls will be able to join hands with little white boys and white girls as sisters and brothers. I have a dream today!

I have a dream that one day every valley shall be exalted, every hill and mountain shall be made low, the rough places shall be made plain, and the crooked places shall be made straight and the glory of the Lord will be revealed and all flesh shall see it together. This is our hope. This is the faith that I go back to the South with.

With this faith we will be able to hew out of the mountain of despair a stone of hope. With this faith we will be able to transform the jangling discords of our nation into a beautiful symphony of brotherhood.

With this faith we will be able to work together, to pray together, to struggle together, to go to jail together, to stand up for freedom together, knowing that we will be free one day. This will be the day when all of God's children will be able to sing with new meaning—"my country 'tis of thee; sweet land of liberty; of thee I sing; land where my fathers died, land of the pilgrim's pride, from every mountain side, let freedom ring"—and if America is to be a great nation, this must become true.

So let freedom ring from the prodigious hilltops of New Hampshire.

Let freedom ring from the mighty mountains of New York.

Let freedom ring from the heightening Alleghenies of Pennsylvania.

Let freedom ring from the snow-capped Rockies of Colorado.

Let freedom ring from the curvaceous slopes of California.

But not only that.

Let freedom ring from Stone Mountain of Georgia.

Let freedom ring from Lookout Mountain of Tennessee.

Let freedom ring from every hill and molehill of Mississippi, from every mountainside, let freedom ring.

And when we allow freedom to ring, when we let it ring from every village and hamlet, from every state and city, we will be able to speed up that day when all of God's children—black men and white men, Jews and Gentiles, Catholics and Protestants—will be able to join hands and to sing in the words of the old Negro spiritual, "Free at last, free at last, thank God Almighty, we are free at last."

When King finished, there was silence at first among the huge throng. Then the crowd went wild with joy. At that moment they felt a collective soul force that was so powerful, it seemed nothing could stop it.

Sadly, the forces of violence and hatred continued to run strong. On September 15 the Sixteenth Street Baptist Church in Birmingham, where the children's campaign had been organized, was bombed, killing four black girls. And on November 22, President John F. Kennedy was assassinated in Dallas, Texas.

The following summer the Student Nonviolent Coordinating Committee launched a massive voter-registration drive in Mississippi and Alabama. SNCC workers were beaten and jailed by the score. The Congress of Racial Equality also planned an action in Mississippi that summer. Two young white CORE workers from the North, Michael Schwerner and Andrew Goodman, and a black civil rights worker from the South, James Chaney, were murdered in Philadelphia, Mississippi.

In October 1964, amidst the violence, Martin Luther King, Jr., was awarded the Nobel Prize for Peace. King, only the second black American to be so honored (the first was Ralph Bunche for his work for peace between Israel and its Arab neighbors in the late 1940s), was chosen to receive the Prize for Peace because of his commitment to nonviolent social change,

Leaders of the march met in 1963 with President John F. Kennedy who drew up a civil rights bill before his assassination in November of that same year.

President Lyndon B. Johnson pushed Kennedy's civil rights bill through Congress. He invited King to the White House in July to witness the signing into law of the landmark Civil Rights Act of 1964.

Martin and Coretta King, along with a group of friends and advisers, traveled to Oslo, Norway, in December to accept the prize. King delivered his acceptance speech before the king of Norway, the Norwegian parliament, and other dignitaries:

Your Majesty, your Royal Highness, Mr. President, excellencies, ladies and gentlemen:

I accept the Nobel Prize for Peace at a moment when twenty-two million Negroes of the United States of America are engaged in a creative battle to end the long night of racial injustice. I accept this award in behalf of a civil rights movement which is moving with determination and a majestic scorn for risk and danger to establish a reign of freedom and a rule of justice.

I am mindful that only yesterday in Birmingham, Alabama, our children, crying out for brotherhood, were answered with fire hoses, snarling dogs and even death. I am mindful that only yesterday in Philadelphia, Mississippi, young people seeking to secure the right to vote were brutalized and murdered.

I am mindful that debilitating and grinding poverty afflicts my people and chains them to the lowest rung of the economic ladder.

Therefore, I must ask why this prize is awarded to a movement which is beleaguered and committed to unrelenting struggle; to a movement which has not won the very peace and brotherhood which is the essence of the Nobel Prize.

After contemplation, I conclude that this award which I receive on behalf of that movement is profound recognition that nonviolence is the answer to the crucial political and moral question of our time—the need for man to overcome oppression and violence without resorting to violence and oppression. . . .

Firemen remove the body of a little girl from the Sixteenth Street Baptist Church in Birmingham. She was one of four black girls killed by a bomb that was thrown through an open window during their Sunday school.

King accepts the Nobel Peace Prize in Oslo, Norway, on behalf of the civil rights movement.

The tactic of nonviolence would be tested more—and soon. In January 1965, only weeks after King had received the Nobel Prize, SNCC decided to hold a massive campaign of demonstrations in Selma, Alabama. King and other SCLC leaders went to Selma hoping to keep the lines of communication with authorities open and to keep the demonstrations and marches nonviolent. But white response to the campaign was so violent that civil rights activists were outraged.

King decided to direct these strong feelings into some positive action and called for a march from Selma to Montgomery, the state capital. The march began on Sunday, March 7. As the marchers tried to cross the Edmund Pettus Bridge, state troopers on horseback charged them with tear gas, bullwhips, and nightsticks. But the marchers did not break ranks, and they did not fight back.

The day came to be called Bloody Sunday—and it shocked the nation. King announced he would lead a peaceful march from Selma to Montgomery. He asked American clergymen, black and white, to join him, and they did, coming from across the country. Two days later a second march began. But it was stalled when troops blocked the road on the far side of the Edmund Pettus Bridge. The march finally began for a third time on March 21, and federal troops protected the marchers. But no one protected Mrs. Viola Liuzzo, a white housewife from Detroit who had volunteered to transport marchers back and forth. While driving a young black civil rights worker, she was shot to death by a carload of Ku Klux Klansmen.

Whether it was the nonviolence of civil rights workers or the violence of white racists, or a combination of the two, the upheaval in the South led to the passage of landmark civil rights legislation in 1964 and 1965. Vice President Lyndon B. Johnson, a Texan, succeeded to the presidency after the assassination of President Kennedy. He made it his personal challenge to see through to passage the civil rights legislation the late president had championed, and he used all his considerable influence on Congress to see that it was passed. The 1964 Civil Rights Act and the 1965 Voting Rights Act essentially

Demonstrators flocked to Selma, Alabama, in 1965.

On March 7, 1965, state troopers beat and tear-gassed marchers as they started over Selma's Edmund Pettus Bridge on their way to Montgomery. This brutal day became known as Bloody Sunday.

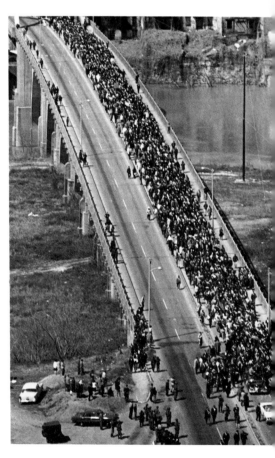

Two days later, after marchers crossed the bridge,
they knelt in prayer and sang "We Shall Overcome."

State troopers blocked the road; the protestors
turned back to Selma.

On March 21, protestors—for the third time—poured
across the Edmund Pettus Bridge.

This time, protected by the National Guard, some three
hundred marchers made the four-day-long trek to Montgomery.
"We are on the move now to the land of freedom."

removed all the legal barriers to equal rights for black people. Slowly and reluctantly, the southern states and localities would comply, but not for a long time. In some rural areas it took until the 1970s for "White" and "Colored" signs to be removed.

While the direct-action civil rights movement in the South came to an end, the need for action against discrimination did not. When blacks in northern and western cities such as Newark, Detroit, and Los Angeles rioted, King and other civil rights leaders realized they had neglected the millions of urban blacks outside the South who suffered from discrimination in education, jobs, and housing.

King tried to take his movement to the cities, organizing marches and demonstrations in Chicago. He was unsuccessful, however. He and Coretta tried moving into slum housing in Chicago, but they did not win much support among ghetto residents. He led a march through Cicero, Illinois, a white working-class suburb of Chicago, and was stoned by white onlookers. As he wrote in his book *Where Do We Go from Here?*, "Jobs are harder and costlier to create than voting rolls. The eradication of slums housing millions is complex far beyond integrating buses and lunch counters." Northern urban blacks did not respond to the idea of nonviolence the way southern blacks had. Instead, they cheered the call for "black power!" issued by the new chairman of SNCC, Stokely Carmichael. After the brutal summer of 1964, many in SNCC had renounced nonviolence, and now these people controlled the organization.

Another militant group was the Nation of Islam, also known as the Black Muslims, whose most charismatic spokesman was Malcolm X, minister of Muslim Temple Number 7 in New York. Malcolm X preached black separatism and black self-determination, and he criticized Martin Luther King for preaching nonviolence, saying it was foolish for blacks to practice nonviolence in the face of such ferocious violence from whites. The two men met only once and liked each other personally, but they continued to disagree on tactics.

King flew to Watts, the black ghetto of Los Angeles that erupted in terrifying riots in the summer of 1965. The angry Watts residents opposed King's doctrine of nonviolence.

King was hit by a rock during a march in Chicago.

King moved with his wife, Coretta, into slum housing on Chicago's West Side.

A street in Detroit's ghetto burns during a 1967 riot. "We still have a choice today: nonviolent coexistence or violent coannihilation. This may well be mankind's last chance to choose between chaos and community."

# "Free at last"

Where do we go from here? was a real question in Martin Luther King's mind. He was an internationally recognized leader who had lost his platform. By 1967 the United States was deeply involved in the Vietnam conflict, and King spoke out against this involvement. He felt the United States was morally wrong to interfere in the affairs of another country; he also felt the United States was relying on its youngest and poorest citizens to fight that war, since the majority were poor, uneducated young men and a disproportionate number were black. His stand against the war brought criticism from both whites and blacks, and he lost some powerful supporters as a result.

Perhaps aware that his strengths lay in speaking on behalf of the downtrodden, King decided to broaden his cause and to speak out not just for poor blacks but for all poor people. Excitedly, he proposed to the other leaders of the SCLC a Poor People's March on Washington in the spring of 1968. He officially announced plans for the march on December 4, 1967, saying that it would be for jobs and for a guaranteed income for everyone not able to work. In short, they would demand a sort of economic Bill of Rights.

In the next few months, King crisscrossed the country urging poor people to join the march and making plans for the event, which was scheduled for April. He really did not have time to visit Memphis, Tennessee, to attend a protest march by striking sanitation workers. But he found it hard to turn down requests from friends, and when the Reverend Billy Kyles asked him to support the workers by joining their march, he consented.

On March 28, King was walking at the head of a long line of marchers through downtown Memphis when he was suddenly pushed forward by a grim-faced black teenager. Young blacks, many armed with sticks and carrying "Black Power!" signs, were moving in on the marchers. Memphis police moved in on them, and soon the planned nonviolent march had dissolved in violence.

In despair, King feared that the nonviolent civil rights movement would suffer a tremendous setback if that violent image was not erased from the public mind. He announced that he would return to Memphis for a peaceful protest. He went to Memphis again on April 3 to prepare for the march, which was planned for April 5. He declined to attend a rally that evening at the local Mason Temple, saying he had telephone calls to make. He was making those calls in his room at the Lorraine Motel when his assistant, the Reverend Ralph David Abernathy, told him that two thousand people had braved pouring rain to attend the rally, expecting him to speak. King agreed to go to the Mason Temple and address the crowd. He had not prepared a speech, and as he talked extemporaneously, his thoughts seemed to settle on the concern for his own safety that he and others had begun to feel lately.

> . . . I left Atlanta this morning, and as we got started on the plane, there were six of us, the pilot said over the public address system, "We are sorry for the delay, but we have Dr. Martin Luther King on the plane. And to be sure that all of the bags were checked, and to be sure that nothing would be wrong with the plane, we had to check

A worried-looking
King led the garbage-
men's strike in
Memphis. A riot
broke up the march.

National Guardsmen
line a street in
Memphis, Tennessee,
on March 29, 1968,
the day after the march
erupted in violence.

out everything carefully. And we've had the plane protected and guarded all night."

And then I got into Memphis. And some began to say the threats, or talk about the threats that were out. What would happen to me from some of our sick white brothers?

Well, I don't know what will happen now. We've got some difficult days ahead. But it doesn't matter with me now. Because I've been to the mountaintop. And I don't mind. Like anybody, I would like to live a long life. Longevity has its place. But I'm not concerned about that now. I just want to do God's will. And He's allowed me to go up to the mountain. And I've looked over. And I've seen the promised land. I may not get there with you. But I want you to know tonight, that we, as a people will get to the promised land. And I'm happy, tonight. I'm not worried about anything, I'm not fearing any man. Mine eyes have seen the glory of the coming of the Lord.

The following evening, April 4, as he prepared to go to dinner at the home of the Reverend Kyles, King went out onto the balcony of the Lorraine Motel to give some last-minute instructions to aides waiting in the parking lot below. A crack split the air, and King fell to the balcony floor, the victim of an assassin's bullet.

On Monday, April 8, after a three-day delay, the march in Memphis that King was supposed to have led took place, with Coretta King and three of their children at the head of the line. After that march, King's body was taken home to Atlanta for a huge funeral. After the church service, his body was taken on a final march in a mule-drawn coffin to Southview Cemetery. A large stone monument was placed atop his grave. The inscription on it reads: "Free at Last, Free at Last, Thank God Almighty, I'm Free at Last."

On April 4, 1968, King was shot down on the balcony of his motel in Memphis. He had returned to the city determined to stage a peaceful demonstration. His shocked aides are pointing to the window from which the fatal shot was fired.

Coretta King
at the funeral
services held
in the Ebenezer
Baptist Church.

Close to a
hundred
thousand
mourners
followed King's
coffin, carried
by an old farm
wagon drawn
by mules,
through the
streets of his
hometown.

The tomb of
Martin Luther
King, Jr., in
Atlanta Georgia.

Two months later, James Earl Ray was captured in London. He pleaded guilty to killing King and was sentenced to ninety-nine years in prison. To this day, doubts exist about whether he acted alone. But so far no conspiracy theory has yet been proved. Ray remains in federal prison, one of the most notorious inmates in America.

Even before Martin Luther King, Jr., was killed at the age of thirty-nine, many changes had occurred for black people in the United States. They exercised their right to vote in large numbers and elected members of their race to important positions in local government. They went beyond asking to be served a cup of coffee and demanded, like the sanitation workers in Memphis, equal pay for equal work. They organized on college campuses and demanded that black history and culture be taught. Facing the possibility of his own death, as he did that night of April 3, 1968, King could be proud that he had reached many of the goals he had set for himself. He had become a minister in order to work for social change, and he had spent almost his entire career as a minister doing that work. He had preached the gospel of nonviolence and had never lost his faith in the power of nonviolence to bring about justice in the most peaceful way. He'd had great dreams and seen at least some of those dreams come true.

In the years since Martin Luther King's death, black Americans have made even greater strides. There are black police chiefs and school board officials in the South. In 1990, L. Douglas Wilder of Virginia became the first black governor of a southern state since the post–Civil War Reconstruction period.

Many big cities, including Los Angeles and New York, have elected black mayors. The Reverend Jesse Jackson, an aide to Dr. King at the time he was shot, has launched serious campaigns for the Democratic presidential nomination and attracted a respectable number of votes.

A sizable black middle class has reaped the rewards of the civil rights movement and the affirmative action policies that President Lyndon Johnson championed before he left office in 1968. Black Americans are more visible in every area of public life, from television to sports, from big business to higher education, in the halls of Congress and the halls of the Pentagon.

If he were alive, Martin Luther King, Jr., would be pleased by these positive changes. But he would feel great sorrow about the persistent poverty of the ghettos, the tragedy of the crack epidemic, the millions of unwed black teenage mothers, and the other evidence that racial discrimination and the legacy of slavery still exist.

Sadly, no other black leader has come along to attract the following or to enjoy the stature of Martin Luther King, Jr. He was a singular leader at a singular time in American history. In recognition of his contribution to America, the United States Congress passed a bill providing for a national holiday in honor of King's birthday. In 1984, President Ronald Reagan signed the bill into law. King thus became the first non-president, as well as the first black, to be so honored.

Through the Martin Luther King, Jr., Center for Nonviolent Social Change in Atlanta, King's widow, Coretta, and his children help keep alive not only his memory but also the ideas for which he died.

# Important Events

**IN THE LIFE OF
MARTIN LUTHER KING, JR.**

1929    Martin Luther King, Jr., is born on January 15 in Atlanta, Georgia.

1948    King graduates from Morehouse College in Atlanta.

1951    King graduates from Crozer Theological Seminary in Chester, Pennsylvania.

1953    Martin Luther King, Jr., marries Coretta Scott.

1954    King becomes pastor of the Dexter Avenue Baptist Church in Montgomery, Alabama.

1955    King receives a Ph.D. in theology from Boston University. The Montgomery bus boycott begins. The Montgomery Improvement Association is formed and King is elected president. Yolanda King is born.

1957    The Southern Christian Leadership Conference is formed, and King is elected president. King speaks about voting rights at the Prayer Pilgrimage for Freedom. Martin Luther King III is born.

1958    King's book *Stride Toward Freedom* is published. He is stabbed in New York City.

1959    King travels to India.

1960    King becomes assistant pastor at the Ebenezer Baptist Church in Atlanta.

1961    Dexter King is born. King organizes a desegregation campaign in Albany, Georgia.

| | |
|---|---|
| 1963 | King is involved in protest in Birmingham, Alabama, and writes "Letter from Birmingham City Jail." He delivers his "I Have a Dream" speech in Washington, D.C. Bernice King is born. |
| 1964 | King is awarded the Nobel Prize for Peace. |
| 1965 | King joins the SCLC for a march from Selma to Montgomery. |
| 1966 | King organizes the James Meredith March Against Fear. |
| 1967 | King makes plans for a Poor People's March on Washington. |
| 1968 | King is assassinated on April 4 in Memphis, Tennessee. |

# Sources for Quotations

**"You are as good as anyone"**

"While I was still too young for school I had already learned something about discrimination. . . ."

From *Stride Toward Freedom,* by Martin Luther King, Jr. Also found in *A Testament of Hope: The Essential Writings and Speeches of Martin Luther King, Jr.,* edited by James M. Washington, page 420.

"I remembered a trip to a downtown shoestore with Father when I was still small. . . ."

From *Stride Toward Freedom.* Also found in *A Testament of Hope,* page 420.

**"An inner urge"**

"I had felt the urge to enter the ministry from my latter high school days . . ."

From *Bearing the Cross: Martin Luther King, Jr., and the Southern Christian Leadership Conference,* by David Garrow, page 39.

"For several days we talked and thought and prayed over each of these matters. . . ."

From *Stride Toward Freedom.* Also found in *A Testament of Hope,* page 422.

### Birmingham: "My feet is real tired, but my soul is rested"

"Without manuscript or notes, I told the story of what had happened to Mrs. Parks. . . ."

From *Stride Toward Freedom*. Also found in *A Testament of Hope*, page 435.

"On a chill morning in the autumn of 1956, an elderly, toil-worn Negro woman in Montgomery, Alabama . . ."

From "The Time for Freedom Has Come," *New York Times Magazine* (September 10, 1961):25ff. Also found in *A Testament of Hope*, page 160.

### "The way of nonviolence"

"Three years ago the Supreme Court of this nation rendered in simple, eloquent and unequivocal language a decision . . ."

From "Give Us the Ballot—We Will Transform the South," *Congressional Record* 103 (May 28, 1957):7822–24. Also found in *A Testament of Hope*, page 197.

"The trip had a great impact on me personally. . . ."

From "My Trip to the Land of Gandhi," *Ebony* (July 1959): 84–86, 88–90, 92. Also found in *A Testament of Hope*, page 25.

### Birmingham: "Now is the time"

"My dear Fellow Clergymen: While confined here in the Birmingham city jail . . ."

From "Letter from Birmingham City Jail," *Why We Can't Wait*. Also found in *A Testament of Hope*, page 289.

### "Fire hoses, snarling dogs, and even death"

"So I say to you, my friends, that even though we must face the difficulties of today and tomorrow . . ."

From *Negro History Bulletin* 21 (May 1968):16–17. Also found in *A Testament of Hope*, page 219.

### "Free at last"

". . . I left Atlanta this morning, and as we got started on the plane, there were six of us . . ."

From *Martin Luther King, Jr: A Documentary . . . Montgomery to Memphis*, edited by Flip Schulke, page 222. Also found in *A Testament of Hope*, page 286.


### Sources for Caption Quotations

From *A Testament of Hope: The Essential Writings and Speeches of Martin Luther King, Jr.*, edited by James M. Washington (San Francisco: HarperCollins Publishers, 1986) and *The Words of Martin Luther King, Jr.*, selected by Coretta Scott King (New York: Newmarket Press, 1983).

# Other Books

**ABOUT MARTIN LUTHER KING, JR.,
AND THE CIVIL RIGHTS MOVEMENT**

Darby, Jean. *Martin Luther King, Jr.* Minneapolis, MN: Lerner
   Publications Co., 1990.

De Kay, James T. *Meet Martin Luther King, Jr.* New York: Random House, 1989.

Faber, Dorris and Harold. *Martin Luther King, Jr.* Englewood
   Cliffs, NJ: Julian Messner, 1986.

Harris, Jacqueline L. *Martin Luther King, Jr.* New York: Franklin Watts, 1983.

Kosof, Anna. *The Civil Rights Movement and Its Legacy.* New
   York: Franklin Watts, 1989.

McKissack, Patricia. *Martin Luther King, Jr. A Man to Remember.*
   Chicago, IL: Childrens Press, 1984.

Parks, Rosa with Haskins, Jim. *Rosa Parks: My Story.* New York:
   The Dial Press, 1991.

Patterson, Lillie. *Martin Luther King, Jr., and the Montgomery
   Bus Boycott.* New York: Facts on File, 1989.


Other books by Jim Haskins

*Amazing Grace: The Story Behind the Song.* Brookfield, CT: The
   Millbrook Press, 1992.

*The Life and Death of Martin Luther King, Jr.* New York: Lothrop, Lee & Shepard Co., 1977.

*On the Day That Martin Luther King, Jr., Was Shot.* New York:
   Scholastic, 1992.

# Selected Bibliography

Abernathy, Ralph David. *And the Walls Came Tumbling Down.* New York: Harper & Row Publishers, 1986.

Beifus, Joan Turner. *At the River I Stand.* Memphis, TN: St. Luke's Press, 1990.

Branch, Taylor. *Parting the Waters: America in the King Years, 1954–63.* New York: Simon & Schuster, 1988.

Frank, Gerold. *An American Death.* New York: Doubleday & Co., 1972.

Garrow, David J. *Bearing the Cross: Martin Luther King, Jr. and the Southern Christian Leadership Conference.* New York: William Morrow & Co., 1986.

King, Martin Luther, Jr. *Stride Toward Freedom.* San Francisco: Harper & Row Publishers, 1958.

King, Martin Luther, Jr. *Where Do We Go from Here: Chaos or Community?* Boston: Beacon Press, 1968.

King, Martin Luther, Jr. *Why We Can't Wait.* New York: New American Library, 1964.

Schulke, Flip, ed. *Martin Luther King, Jr.: A Documentary . . . Montgomery to Memphis.* New York: W. W. Norton & Co., 1976.

Schulke, Flip, and Penelope O. McPhee. *King Remembered.* New York: W. W. Norton & Co., 1986.

Washington, James M., ed. *A Testament of Hope: The Essential Writings and Speeches of Martin Luther King, Jr.* San Francisco: HarperCollins Publishers, 1986.

# Index

Mays, Benjamin, 26
Montgomery bus boycott
    (1955–1956), *36*, 37–40, *41*,
    42, *43*, 44, *45*, *46*, 47
Montgomery Improvement As-
    sociation (MIA), *36*, 37–40,
    42, 44, 49
Morehouse College, Atlanta,
    Ga., 14, 25–26, *28*
Muslim Temple Number 7,
    New York, N.Y., 88
Muste, A. J., 27

NAACP (National Association
    for the Advancement of Col-
    ored People), 35, 53
Nation of Islam, 88, *91*
New England Conservatory of
    Music, Boston, Ma., 30
Nobel Prize for Peace, 80, 82,
    *83*
Nonviolence and civil disobe-
    dience, 27, *28*, 29, 39, 40, *43*,
    *48*, 53, *54*, 55, 82, 84, 88, *90*,
    94, 100
North Carolina College, 55

Parks, Rosa, 7–10, 37, 38, *41*
Poor People's March on Wash-
    ington (1968), 93–94
Prayer Pilgrimage for Freedom
    (1957), 50, *51*

Randolph, A. Philip, 75
Ray, James Earl, 100
Reagan, Ronald, 101
Reddick, Lawrence D., 53
Rustin, Bayard, 75

Schwerner, Michael, 80

SCLC (Southern Christian
    Leadership Conference), 49–
    50, 52, 59, 61, 64, 73, 84, 93
Selma to Montgomery marches
    (1965), 84, *85–87*
Shaw University, 55
Sixteenth Street Baptist
    Church, Birmingham, Ala.,
    bombing (1963), 80, *83*
SNCC (Student Nonviolent Co-
    ordinating Committee), 55,
    59, 80, 84, 88, *91*
*Stride Toward Freedom* (King),
    17, 53, *54*
Supreme Court of the United
    States, 35, 44, *46*, 50, 67

Thoreau, Henry David, 27

Vietnam War, 93
Voting rights, 49–50, *51*, *52*,
    84, 100
Voting Rights Act (1965), 84

Washington, Booker T., 39–40
Watts riots (1965), *89*
*Where Do We Go From Here?*
    (King), 88
White Citizens Council, 42, *43*,
    *66*
Wilder, L. Douglas, 100
Williams, Adam Daniel, 13
Williams, Mama (grand-
    mother), 14
Women's College of North Car-
    olina, 55

Young, Andrew, 62

Zerg, James, *58*

## PHOTOGRAPHS COURTESY OF: